C000001937

Purple Ronnie's Star Signs

Aquarius

20th January - 18th February

☆

First published 1994 by Statics(London)Ltd

This edition published 2002 by Boxtree
an imprint of Pan Macmillan Ltd
Pan Macmillan, 20 New Wharf Road, London N1 9RR
Basingstoke and Oxford
Associated companies throughout the world
www.panmacmillan.com

ISBN 0 7522 6183 5

9 8 7 6 5 4 3 2 1

A CIP catalogue record for this book is available from
the British Library

Text by Giles Andreae
Illustrations by Janet Cronin
Printed and bound in Hong Kong

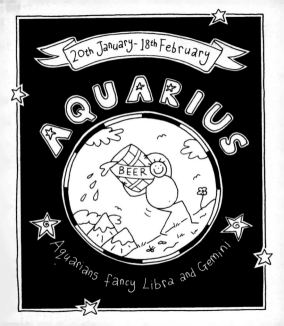

☆ Introduction ☆

Star Signs are a brilliant way of finding out about someone's character. You can use them to discover anything you like including what everyone's secretest rude fantasies are.

But reading what's written in the stars can only be done by incredibly brainy people like me. After gazing for ages through my gigantic telescope and doing loads of complicated sums and charts and stuff I have been able to work out exactly what everyone in the world is really like.

This book lets you know about all my amazing discoveries. It tells you what you look like, who your friends are, how your love life is, what you're like at Doing It and who you should be Doing It with. Everything I've written in this book is completely true. Honest.

Love from

Purple Ronnie

xox

Contents

They're bad at expressing
their feelings
And bottle them all up
inside
But when they're in
love
They say "Heavens
above
I'm all wonky and
googly-eyed"

Aquarius Looks

If you see someone who looks like they have just landed from another planet you are probably looking at an Aquarius

Aquarius Men

Aquarius Men have a big friendly happy smile. They often go bald quickly and they love dressing up in girls' undies

<u>Aquarius Women</u>

Aquarius Women look incredibly gorgeous and totally weird at the same time. They don't like normal clothes so they often dress in loony styles

Aquarius Character

Aquarius people are totally unique. They think in crazy ways that no-one else understands and they are often miles ahead of their time

Aquarians love having loads of ideas about changing the world

Aquarius and Friends

Aquarian people are fun
to muck around with...

...and they always have a groovy mixture of friends

But they are not very good...

...if you want to sit down on your own with them and sort out all your problems

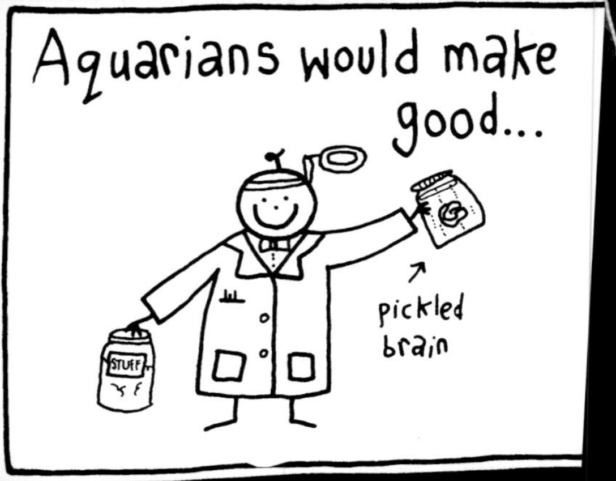
Aquarians would make good...
STUFF
pickled brain

1. They love science and gadgets and anything to do with the future

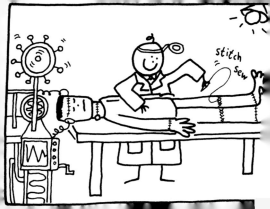

2. They hate normal jobs and are often best at working on their own

3. They look at everything they come across in a new way

CONDOMS

Aquarius and Love

Aquarians who look for love will want someone who will understand the way they think

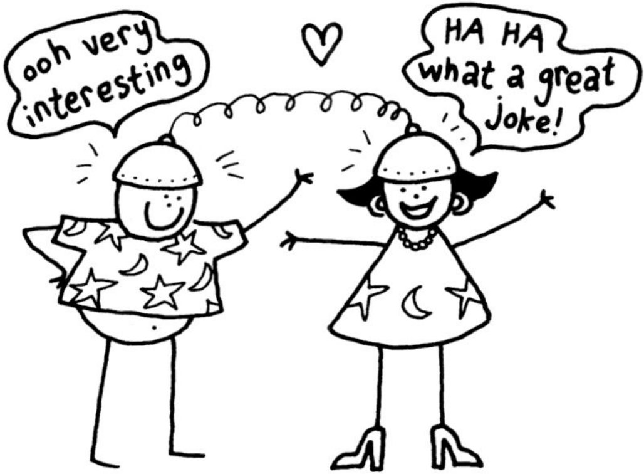
ooh very interesting
HA HA what a great joke!

Warning:-

Aquarius people hate talking about their own feelings but they love finding out about yours

The more space you give an Aquarius to do their own thing the more they will love you

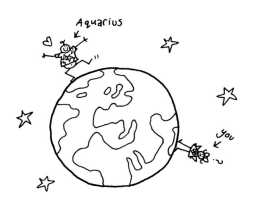

This can be quite difficult

Aquarius and Sex

Aquarians are brilliant at snogging...

...but when it comes to Doing It they get all shy and embarrassed

☆ Special Tip ☆

If you want to Do It with an Aquarian you must tell them it's their brains you fancy them for

Sex with
an Aquarian
is never
normal

The End